Windows of the World

Other books by Jean-Philippe and Dominique Lenclos:
Colors of the World
Doors of the World
Couleurs de la France
Couleurs de l'Europe

Windows of the World

Jean-Philippe and Dominique Lenclos

Foreword by Tom Porter

W. W. Norton & Company
New York • London

To Peter Keller

Originally published in French as FENÊTRES DU MONDE

Printed in Italy

Translated by Andrea Costella
Manufacturing by Rotolito Lombarda
Book design by Philippe Millot
Production manager: Leeann Graham

Library of Congress Cataloging-in-Publication Data

Lenclos, Jean-Philippe.
[Fenêtres du monde. English]
Windows of the world / Jean-Philippe and Dominique Lenclos.
p. cm.
ISBN 0-393-73188-X (pbk.)
1. Windows. I. Lenclos, Dominique. II. Title.

NA3020 .L4613 2005
721'.823—dc22 2005047312

W. W. Norton & Company, Inc., 500 Fifth Avenue, New York, N.Y. 10110
www.wwnorton.com
W. W. Norton & Company Ltd., Castle House, 75/76 Wells St., London W1T 3QT

0 9 8 7 6 5 4 3 2 1

Foreword

Emerging as it does from Jean-Philippe and Dominique Lenclos's well-documented investigations into architectural color—encapsulated in their book, *Colors of the World* (Norton, 2004)—*Windows of the World* is the companion volume to *Doors of the World* and completes their study of the two key features of a habitat's facade. The Lenclos's study results from a research program that is both simple and logical. First, selecting sites typical of a region and armed with the knowledge that traditional settlements are built from the substrate upon which they stand, they take color samples of locally applied pigment from each architectural component of a habitat, in addition to its building materials and the structure's indigenous flora and local geology. Later, back in their studio, the samples are meticulously color matched in gouache and assembled into color palettes, which are classified to represent facades and architectural details. The resulting palettes then function as a design tool, able to be applied to both existing and proposed architecture. Initially, the Lenclos's research led to a series of commissions in which they were asked to provide color maps for various French towns, including Creteuil and Cergy-Pontoise, as well as for countless traditional settlements across France. Later, enthusiastically adopted by the Japanese Color Planning Center in Tokyo, the Lenclos turned their attention to a broader, more international spectrum, establishing themselves as the leading colorists of Europe, if not the world.

The original intention behind the Lenclos's color-mapping method was to serve as an antidote to the relentless proliferation of a gray, concrete architecture that threatened to dilute traditional color systems. In this age of globalization, their work confronts the threat of the universal and uniform culture and supports their mission to document and defend the incidence of local architectural color along an international spectrum. Armed with recording equipment, including a camera, color swatches, colored pencils, watercolors, and a penknife (to extract flakes of indigenous paint and building materials), the Lenclos have traveled into the sunlight of many continents. Their studies of the architectural facade and its apertures form the basis of this book.

As an architectural space-framing device, the window separates viewer from view, inside from outside, and public from private to select and isolate the scene beyond. Although the translucency of window glass is associated with enigma and ambiguity for what lies beyond, its transparency and the dual revelation of reflection and visual access is deeply significant in Modernist thinking. The shape of the window was also the subject of a controversy in 1923 between Auguste Perret and Le Corbusier concerning framing with horizontal or vertical windows: Perret's preference for vertical windows permits a perspective view that includes foreground and background, whereas the horizontal window, which removes these depth cues, denies depth and wallpapers the panorama to the glass.

Windows are often described as the eyes of a building, which leads us to its two-part role in revealing and framing spectacles—from the inside, the spectacle of the street, and, after nightfall, the almost cinematic spectacle of life played out from within. This role is celebrated to the full in the intricate decorations traditionally found in different cultures and so beautifully illustrated here. Like their optical counterparts, window apertures admit light while allowing a framed view of the outside world. Like eyelids, external blinds, shutters, and awnings filter, shade, and block sunlight. These window elements all become a sort of eye cosmetic, pigment being traditionally applied to celebrate and enhance their existence on a wall. But this elaboration can also involve practicality. For example, the widespread use of white on frames and on reveals, especially in more northern climes, traditionally encourages not only a contrasting decoration but improves the amount of internal illumination. This ploy is similar to the one used by Le Corbusier on his Unité d'Habitation in Marseilles, where his insertion of primary colors on window reveals modifies deflected sunlight to tinge the interior space beyond. Certain hues can also be specific to rural communities based on regional traditions and mores, like the frames of farmhouse windows in Switzerland and Italy, for example, which are painted either blue or yellow following a folklore that dictates that these colors will, in summertime, inhibit the influx of flies through open windows.

Windows also define a zone that, from the outside, creates its own miniature, boxed landscape. On the inside, this zone provides a transitional place where the inhabitant can reflect and enjoy having a kind of "private eye," secret access to a surrounding but detached world—the voyeuristic gaze often betrayed by a twitching curtain. Gio Ponti once said, "Tombs have windowless fronts because no one will ever look out from them; windows represent life, the life inside."

By celebrating the window in all its forms and hues, this book culminates over three decades of intrepid research by the authors in the study of architectural color—a discipline widely ignored in educational design establishments. *Windows of the World* reaffirms that the vocabulary of color is alive and well in the traditional built environment, its incidence revealed by the basic urge to decorate, to signify pride of place, ownership, and individuality, and to reflect the hues and local belief systems that are natural to a region.

Tom Porter

Preface

After three books dedicated to the color of vernacular habitats in France, Europe, and the rest of the world, it struck us as opportune to examine the major components of houses. This study looks at windows.

Indeed, architecture is essentially founded on the composition of functional elements, such as doors, which give access to the interior of the house, and windows or other openings, which allow light to enter into a home and its inhabitants to watch, through them, what happens outside.

If you were to compare a house to a human face, the door, subject of a companion volume, is the mouth (in fact, in a number of African languages, the door is referred to as "the mouth of the house"); the windows are the eyes, protected by the eyelids—shutters or other coverings that open, open part way, or are closed.

We are interested in the elements that appeal to designers, architects, colorists, and, more generally, to everyone sensitive to architectural nuance, no matter how modest. Like our previous studies, this book purposely distances itself from the monumental, whether civil or religious architecture.

From the various countries we visited, we have selected aspects of certain openings that interest us: in some places, it is the design and proportion; in others, the particular character of the relationship between colors; in others still, the poetry conveyed when inhabitants embellish and personalize their windows with plants or carefully chosen curtains, for example. The style of a window is an equally important factor to consider because it expresses and reveals the architectural vocabulary of a given time.

The images we have selected seek to emphasize what is sometimes misunderstood, even mistaken, but basically too often ignored by inhabitants themselves—the harmony born from a balance of proportion, design, material, and color. The images do not constitute an exhaustive or theoretical study of windows.

The approach here is really the point of view of ordinary passersby attentive to the built environment. We gathered images from here and there according to significant elements and what would pique interest, admiration, or emotion. This collection is therefore personal and subjective.

This book is the result of an often difficult selection: too many windows find themselves in the way of pipes, electric cables, or unfortunate transformations effected by the inhabitant. Our photographs rarely assemble all the aspects of an ideal door, but offer an idea of the theme's rich variations. This infinite richness is testimony to the creative genius of architects, artisans, and inhabitants themselves, in a historic, geographic, and cultural context.

This ensemble of vignettes demonstrates in a simple fashion the colors of twenty-five houses from Bonnieux, in the Vaucluse region of France.

The various woodwork tonalities stand out against the sand-colored palette of the facades. For the most part, window frame colors are similar to those used on doors, but lighter in tone.

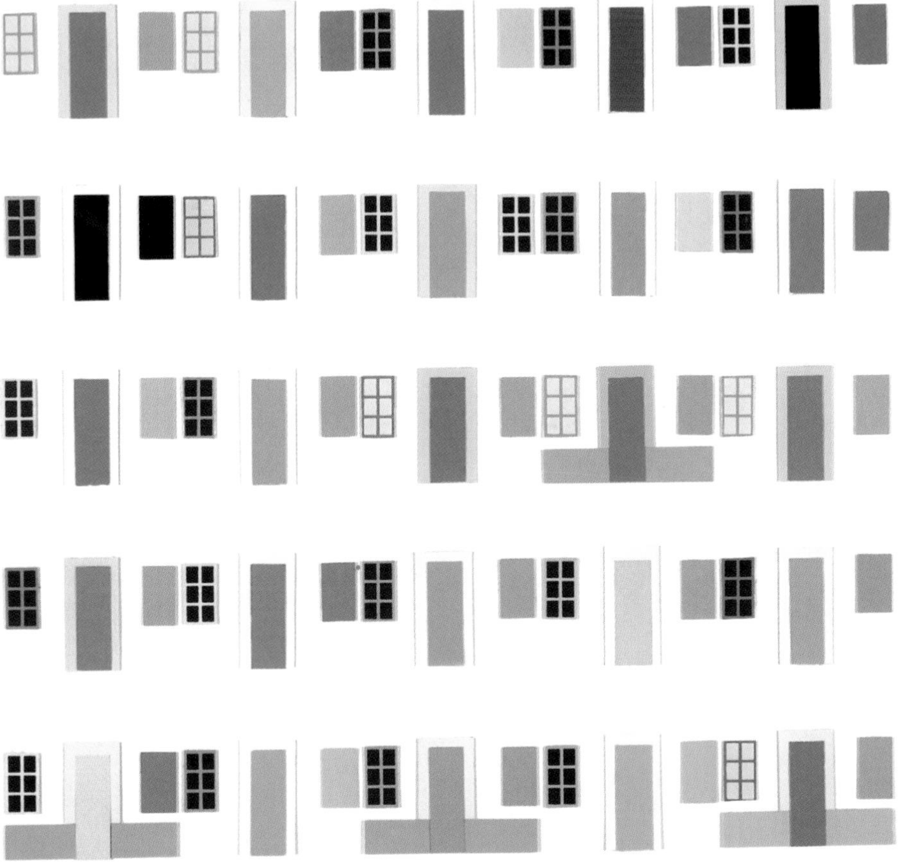

Windows

Windows are openings found on the facades of every type of habitat, from the most modest to the most extravagant.

In fact, the most basic home in Brazil, composed of a simple square pierced with a door and a window, is known as a "door-and-window" house.

While a door allows for passage, a window has multiple functions: it lets daylight enter the home while protecting it from the weather and noise; it permits a certain amount of ventilation; it allows its inhabitants to observe the goings-on outside, whether the activities of people on the street or the changing seasons. In Japan, for example, sliding windows open wide onto gardens and bring the garden, in a sense, into the home.

The principal function of the window is to ensure communication with the surrounding world from the exterior to the interior, but also from the interior to the exterior.

In certain European countries, the decor of a carefully laid out room seen through a window is a call to neighbors or an address to passersby to slow down and admire the harmonious, thoughtful composition. Still other windows attract attention thanks to their exterior ornament, such as vines, wisteria, or climbing rose bushes, to which are sometimes added, in Greece or Portugal, one or two bird cages. These temporary elements, though diverse and charming, have nothing to do with the architecture itself, but nevertheless reflect the lifestyle, taste, and character of the inhabitant while adding to the beauty of the facade and the animation of the urban space. Just as you can consider the doorway the "mouth" of the house, windows, whether accompanied by shutters or not, are its eyes, more or less open, more or less luminous and inviting.

Windows came later than doors in history, the latter being responsible for the existence of the habitat itself. The oldest windows probably date from neolithic times but, up until relatively recently, they were not found in all civilizations. They spread progressively starting in the late Middle Ages, beginning with religious edifices and lordly residences. In the fifteenth century, mullion windows, which consisted of a superimposition of frames, began to appear. In the eighteenth century, thanks to technological progress, the window was made of two parts that fitted together and eliminated the central mullion. During this time glass windowpanes replaced oiled paper.

When you consider the architectural quality of a house or an ensemble of houses, the openings, and windows in particular, play an essential role in the physiology of the facade, imprinting it with a specific dimension, form, style, and accessory, a character appropriate to its time and place. Windows strongly contribute to the local identity of a habitat and create a sense of harmony that makes the home distinct.

The prevailing window composition in classical architecture is a series of rectangles stacked in decreasing size from the ground floor up (when the ground floor is considered the principal floor, which is the case in homes in the countryside). The rectangles are taller than they are wide and their form evokes the stature of a standing man. As long as traditional building materials were used, this form evolved very little. The width of the rectangle did not exceed the width of the two window panels and corresponded to the length of the lintel, which was made of a single piece of stone or wood. Thanks to their clean punctuation, dormer windows and oculi eventually added to the architectural ornament of windows.

The appearance of new materials eliminated some technical constraints and allowed the construction of large, glassed-in bay windows, which seem to bring the countryside into the home.

Window frames and posts, which for centuries were made of wood, are now often replaced by vinyl or aluminum, which resist weathering better but do not offer the material and structural qualities that naturally weathered wood does, thus requiring regular touch-ups in colors that complement local traditions.

Shutters not only serve as protection against curious passersby and potential burglars, especially at night, but protect the house from cold and wind in northern climates and from heat and strong sun in southern climates where, during the traditional siesta, closed shutters bring in a soft light conducive to sleep, while allowing the breeze to enter.
The earliest shutters, appearing in lordly residences of the sixteenth century, were interior. The shutter then moved to the exterior, thereby also protecting windowpanes from wind and rain. While some northern countries do without shutters, other countries, especially those in the south, are quite fond of them.

Several different types of shutters exist. Wooden shutters are generally made of thick, vertical planks of wood, supported by two or three crosspieces, also made of wood. A Z-shaped crosspiece helps to maintain the stability of lighter planks. Louvered shutters, originating in Italy at the end of the eighteenth century, consist of slats of wood fixed to a frame; they open to allow for ventilation. These shutters may include a removable blind to regulate the intensity of the light coming in, in order to see without being seen. Shutter woodwork, like that of doors, strongly contributes to the visual identity of the local, regional, or national habitat.

Metal shutters soon replaced wooden shutters; in turn, metal shutters were joined by rolling shutters, practically invisible when raised, and by plastic shutters that imitate wooden louvers. Central heating, double-glazed windows, and air-conditioning are making shutters less useful and may ultimately lead to their disappearance altogether.

However, the presence of shutters is so viscerally inscribed in our hearts that in the United States, for example, imitation shutters are affixed to the facade of some prefabricated homes to act as a sort of decorative element.

The color of windows and shutters, like the color of doors, adds emphasis and attracts the attention of passersby, as well as guests who come for the first time: "You can't miss it. It's the house with the blue shutters." Color is not dictated by decorative concern only, the paint being primarily used as protection for the woodwork. Esthetic and utilitarian concerns combine harmoniously to give each facade its unique character.

This chart presents an inventory of shutter colors taken from twenty-nine sites in France. A color synthesis chart, it illustrates the concept of the "geography of color," a system through which we can characterize the habitats of every country and every region by a unique chromatic palette.

France

In France, as is the case in the majority of countries around the world, the window is the element that determines the typology of a habitat. If you were to perform a cursory survey of vernacular architecture, you would notice that very often a mere glance at the architectural "language" of a window reveals its region or its village of origin.

The form and the type of woodwork, the number and the proportion of the casements, the design of the shutters, and the color of the paint are all important elements in determining the regional identification of a window.

Moreover, the cut of the window frame, the kinds of materials that surround the window—those of the frame and those of the house's facade—are significant reference points: if granite surrounds the window, Brittany comes to mind; tuffeau, you think of countries in the Loire region; red brick recalls northern France or Pas-de-Calais.

No matter what the region, the window frame (like the door frame) almost always serves as the object of particular attention in marking the opening. In countries where stone is the dominant material, the window frame is defined by the assembly of carefully shaped stone that stand out from a stonework masonry, coated or uncoated. In countries where brick is used, in the north, only the lintel appears, while in the southwest, a frame of exposed bricks outlines the openings. The beauty and charm of a window not only derives from its proportions and the care taken in its framing but also from the choice of shutters. Indeed, in France, most windows are ornamented with shutters.

Traditionally made of wood, shutters differ according to region: in central France, they are composed of two grooved planks placed opposite each other, following an ancient method. In most other regions, shutters are composed of a single plank connected by two or three horizontal crosspieces.

Solid shutters are sometimes pierced with hearts, as in Béarn, clovers, as in the Savoy region, or other motifs or symbols, as in Alsace. Sometimes, if left in its natural state, woodwork assumes a gray tint as it weathers, but it is generally painted to protect it from weathering.

Color is thus no longer simply a decorative element, but a sort of necessary covering through which, in certain regions, a traditional respect for specific hues manifests itself: green in Alsace and Picardy; red and green in the Basque region; gray in the Loire region; and blue in Brittany.

The proliferation of suburbs has tended to diminish the character of vernacular architecture. Some architects, however, have tried to reestablish elements particular to a certain locale, and have paid attention to the shapes, proportions, and colors of a region's windows. And under pressure from architects and national preservation organizations, engineers have produced materials that employ modern construction methods while retaining a habitat's regional characteristics. In this way, neutral vinyl windows and shutters are being superseded by a higher quality of colors and proportion.

Lower Normandy/Calvados

Brittany/Côtes-d'Armor

Lower Normandy/Calvados

Brittany/Finistère

Rhone-Alps/Haute-Savoie

Provence-Alps-Côte d’Azur/Var

Bourgogne/Saône-et-Loire

North-Pas-de-Calais/Pas-de-Calais

North-Pas-de-Calais/Pas-de-Calais

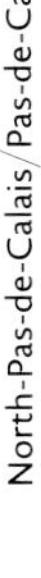

North-Pas-de-Calais/Pas-de-Calais

Picardy/Somme

Brittany/Côtes-d'Armor

Brittany/Côtes-d'Armor

Brittany/Côtes-d'Armor

Brittany/Morbihan/Ile-aux-Moines

Brittany/Morbihan/Ile-aux-Moines

Brittany/Morbihan/Ile-aux-Moines

Brittany/Côtes-d'Armor

Brittany/Morbihan/1980–2000

Bourgogne/Côte-d'Or

Pays de la Loire/Maine-et-Loire

Bourgogne/Côte-d'Or

Pays de la Loire/Maine-et-Loire

Centre/Loir-et-Cher

Centre/Indre-et-Loire

Pays de la Loire/Maine-et-Loire

Provence-Alps-Côte d'Azur / Alps-Maritimes

Midi-Pyrenees/Aveyron

Aquitaine/Dordogne

Ile-de-France/Paris

Ile-de-France/Paris

Ile-de-France/Paris

Ile-de-France/Paris

Europe

Whether in an urban or rural setting, a home's windows often make one think of eyes—open or closed, somber or luminous, underlined with a trace of contrasting color, obscured by a fine lace curtain, or hiding behind closed shutters, unless they're hiding behind an open grille, an invading Virginia creeper, or pots of geraniums—"eyes" so different from one European country to another that, by studying them, it is easy to identify their nationality.

Tracing styles from northern to southern Europe, we will try to define several traits of windows whose look and position on the facade vary according to climate, light intensity, and local building material. If you observe a row of adjoining facades in an old quarter in Copenhagen, Amsterdam, or a small Bavarian village, you will notice that the importance of windows is measured by the architectural framework and the specific morphology of their northern European urban habitat. In Copenhagen, contrasting facade colors contribute to the rhythm of the architectural space and the repetitive punctuation of windows on the facade conveys a framework characteristic of Denmark. In Amsterdam, natural brick, when left to its original color and material, which is marked with holes and other aberrations, delicately frames a fine white-bordered window. In Bavaria, in Wangen, or in Rothenburg, white windows stand out thanks to the attentive care given their freshly painted green or brown shutters, flowerboxes filled with red and green geraniums, and sometimes an elegant Germanic decoration painted on the lintel.

In southern European countries, where windows are generally smaller for weather-related reasons, window ornament is often more discreet in its dimensions and treatment, particularly when shutters, whose visual impact is always very strong, are placed in the interior. This observation applies to the "pueblos blancos" (white villages) of Andalusia, certain villages in the Grecian Islands, or the Italian island of Procida, off the coast of Naples. On the other hand, in Burano, an island of fishermen in the Venetian lagoon, windows framed in white with green shutters, whose tones correspond to strict local traditions, have a striking impact on the alignment of multicolored facades that are reflected in the water of the canals. Blind slats or floral curtains, the charming blossoming of geranium pots on windowsills, lines of hanging clothes that swing gaily from side to side, all are elements that equally contribute to the charm and poetry of these magical places. In Greece, Mykonos illustrates its utterly individual character thanks to the treatment of its openings: doors, windows, and wooden balconies—all painted in the same color, blue, green, ochre, or red—stand out distinctively against the squared, dazzling white facades of the island's simple homes.

These quick observations only offer a cursory view of the extent to which the diverse European countries reveal themselves through their habitats, in particular through windows. Indeed, windows express the richness of all local, regional, and national traditions.

Belgium/Roeselare

Belgium/Bruges

Belgium/Bruges

Belgium/Bruges

Belgium/Bruges

Belgium/Bruges

Belgium/Bruges

Belgium/Bruges

Netherlands/Amsterdam

Netherlands/Marken

Netherlands/Middelburg

Netherlands/Marken

Netherlands/Marken

Netherlands/Marken

Netherlands/Veere

Netherlands/Middelburg

Netherlands/Middelburg

Switzerland/Grindelwald

Switzerland/Grindelwald

Germany/Dinkelsbühl

Germany/Krefeld

Germany/Dinkelsbühl

Germany/Dinkelsbühl

Germany/Dinkelsbühl

Germany/Dinkelsbühl

Germany/Wangen

Germany/Dinkelsbühl

Denmark/Ile de Bornholm

Denmark/Ile de Bornholm

Denmark/Ile de Bornholm

Finland/Porvoo

Finland/Porvoo

Finland/Porvoo

Finland/Porvoo

Russia/Souzdal

Russia/Souzdal

Russia/Souzdal

Russia/Zagorsk

Russia/Souzdal

Russia/Souzdal

Russia/Souzdal

Scotland/Cullen

Scotland/Portnockie

Scotland/Portnockie

Scotland/Cullen

Scotland/Cullen

Scotland/Crovie

Scotland/Crovie

Ireland/Toormore

Ireland/Sneem

Ireland/Eyeries

Ireland/Clonakilty

England/London

England/London

Portugal/Aveiro

Portugal/Alcantarilha

Portugal/Luz de Tavira

Portugal/Luz de Tavira

Portugal/Costa Nova

Portugal/Costa Nova

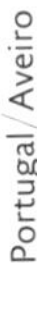

Portugal/Aveiro

Portugal/Costa Nova

Portugal/Costa Nova

Portugal/Costa Nova

Portugal/Amarante

Portugal/Tavira

Portugal/Coimbra

Portugal/Povoa de Varzim

Portugal/Aveiro

Portugal/Povoa de Varzim

Spain/New Castille/Consuegra

Spain/Andalusia/Grazalema

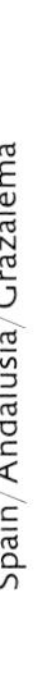

Spain/Andalusia/Grazalema

Italy/Burano

Italy/Burano

Italy/Burano

Italy/Burano

Italy/Burano

Italy/Burano

Italy/Burano

Italy/Burano/Corte Comare

Italy/Procida

Italy/Procida

Italy/Procida

Italy/Procida

Greece/Chios/Pyrghi

Greece/Chios/Pyrghi

Greece/Chois/Pyrghi

Greece/Karpathos/Arkasa

Greece/Karpathos/Olympus

Around the World

Reflecting on the specificities of windows beyond Europe, we can separate them into two distinct groups: those that directly inherited methods of use and construction from old western traditions, and those that were spontaneously born from the needs of a region's population and its local materials.

It is inevitable that, gradually, as Europeans moved to other parts of the world, they brought with them their architectural conceptions and artisanal techniques, which spread progressively, beginning with public buildings and decisively influencing local construction methods. Thus, in New York, for example, it is sometimes difficult to say how a window in Greenwich Village differs from a window in London or Amsterdam. In Salvador de Bahia, Brazil, you can sometimes detect the influence of the old quarters of Porto or Aveiro in Portugal. In Antigua in Guatemala, windows protected by wrought-iron grilles unequivocally recall the traditional architecture of southern Spain. Undoubtedly, several details stick out to differentiate the treatment of architectural elements that have a similar architectural "language." Among these details are the particular interpretation of decor and ornament and the chromatic range, which are very specific to each country.

Certain countries demonstrate an architectural language that is radically different from Europe. This is notably the case in Japan, with its modular wood construction and sliding doors that hide behind *noren*, a window curtain made of two or three parts that are decorated with, for example, a corporate emblem.

In Rajasthan, India, houses in Jaipur or Jaisalmer often evoke the palace of Prince Rajput, with finely carved windows and stone balconies delicately sculpted according to a technique described in Sanskrit canonical manuals that date from more than two thousand years ago.

In Morocco, residential architecture, no matter how important the residence is, is turned towards the interior: the walls are thick, the lateral walls with windows are screened, diffusing light throughout the room, and interior shutters open along a bias cut. The few windows that pierce the facade are protected by *mashrabiya* that diffuse a soft light and simultaneously allow a breeze to enter, while maintaining the family's privacy. Remarkably, in modern areas of Ouarzazate, recent homes that have adopted larger and more numerous openings on the facade still retain the *mashrabiya*, now often made of metal.

South Africa/Free State/Clarens

South Africa/Free State/Clarens

South Africa/Free State/Clarens

South Africa/Free State

South Africa/Free State

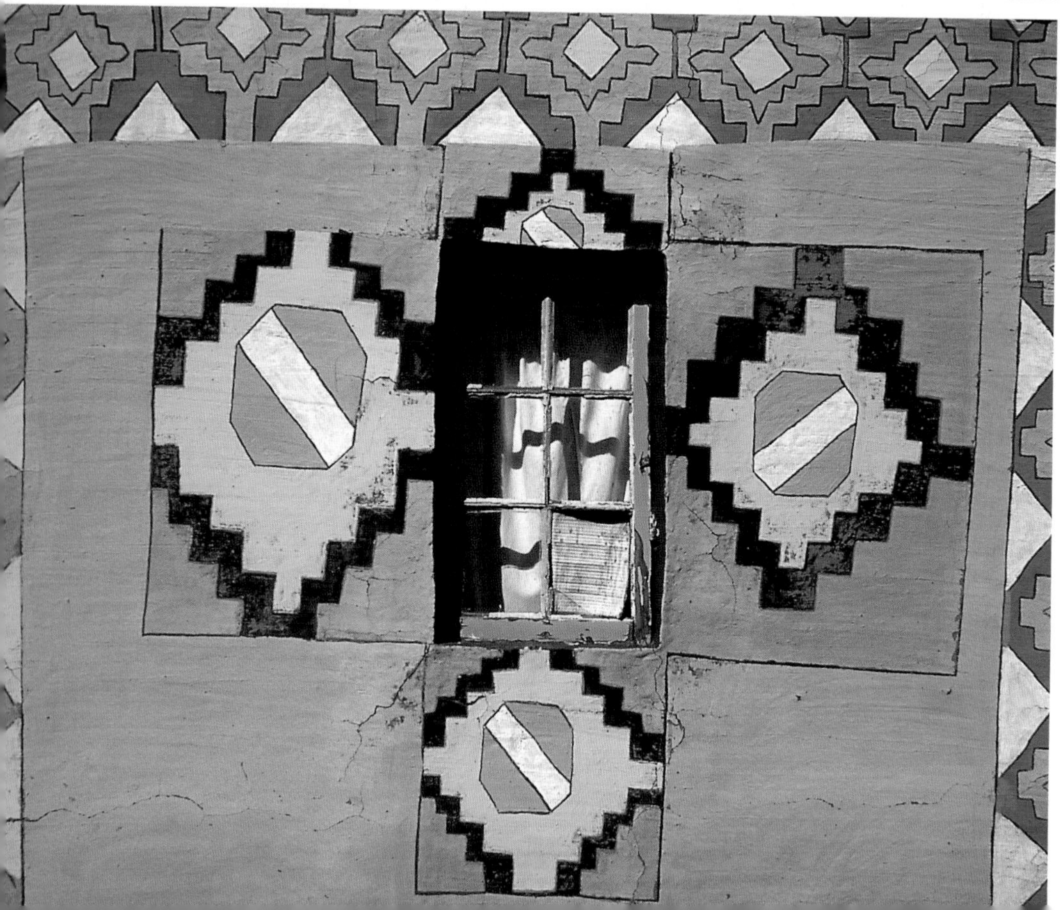

South Africa/Free State

South Africa/Free State

South Africa/Loupoort

South Africa/Loupoort

Egypt/Gournah

Egypt/Louxor

Egypt/East Assouan

Egypt/East Assouan

North Yemen/Kawkaban

North Yemen/Wadi Dhar

North Yemen/Manakha

North Yemen/Sanaa

North Yemen/Wadi Dhar

North Yemen/Manakha

India/Rajasthan/Jaipur

India/Rajasthan/Jaisalmer

India/Rajasthan/Thar Desert

India/Rajasthan/Jodhpur

पं. महेशचन्द्र व्यास एम.ए.
व्यास
परिवार
आपका हार्दि
स्वागत करता

India/Rajasthan/Jodhpur

India/Rajasthan/Jaisalmer

Japan/Murotsu

Japan/Kyoto

Japan/Murotsu

Japan/Murotsu

Japan/Kyoto

Japan/Murotsu

Japan/Kyoto

China/Anhui/Tangkou

China/Anhui/Xidi

China/Huang Shan/Yixian

China/Shanghai

Brazil/Bahia/Salvador

Brazil/Paudalho

Brazil/Alianca

Brazil/Salvador

Brazil/Salvador

Brazil/Paudalho

Brazil/Olinda

Brazil/Paudalho

Brazil/Cachoeira

United States / New York / Greenwich Village

United States/New York/West 94th Street

United States/New York/Greenwich Village

United States/New York/Greenwich Village

United States/New York/Greenwich Village

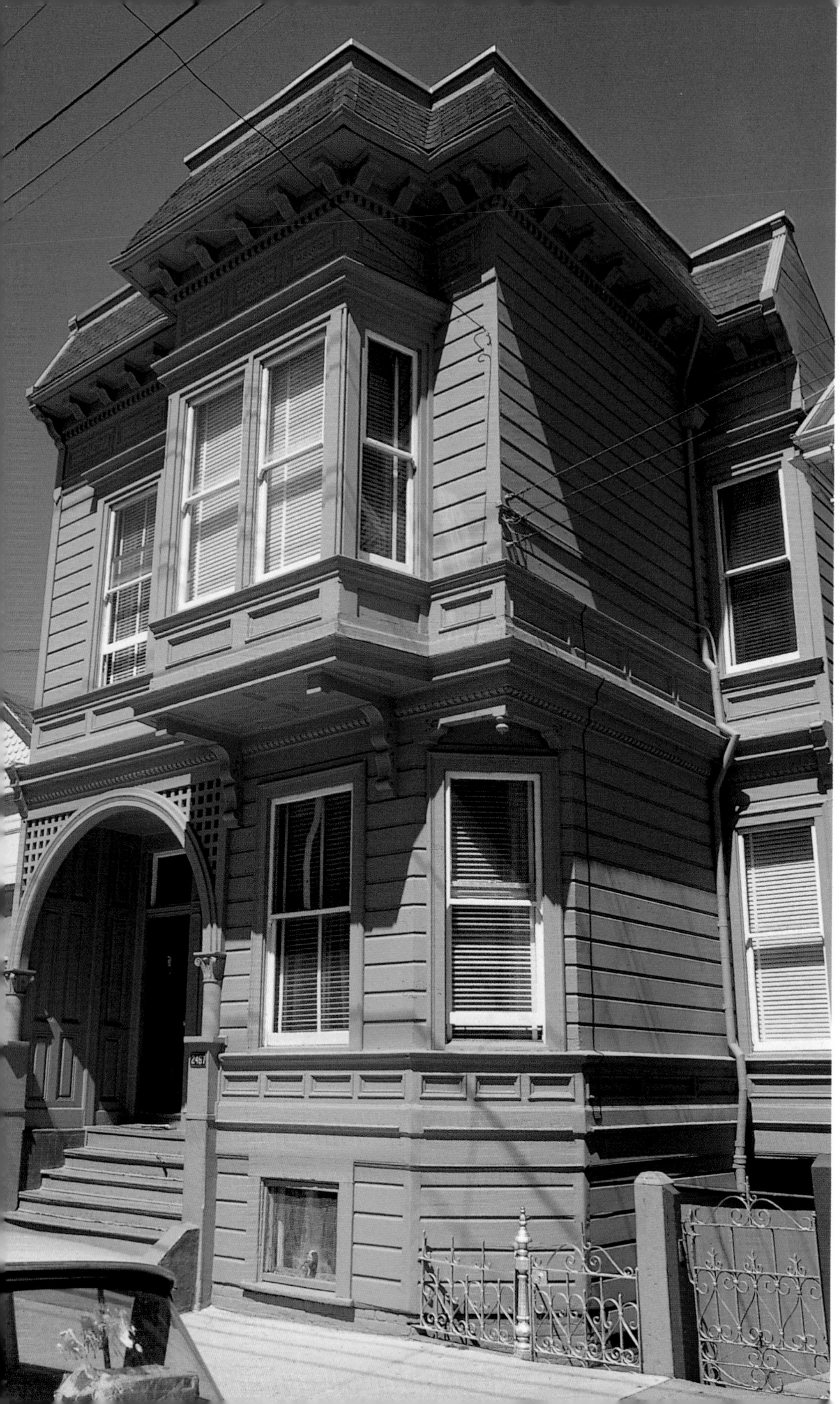

United States/San Francisco

Credits

Photographs: In this book, 174 photographs are taken by Jean-Philippe Lenclos; all others were taken by:

Dominique Lenclos, pages 18, 26, 28, 29, 30, 47, 92, 95, 96, 97, 98, 101, 102, 103, 124, 128, 130, 131, 133, 134, 135, 138, 140, 141, 144, 147, 151a & b, 158, and 164.

Emmanuel Lenclos, pages 56, 91, and 99.

Annie Mayer, page 153.

Illustrations: René Robert, pages 10, 11, and 16.